BROCKWAY TRUCKS
1948 THROUGH 1961
PHOTO ARCHIVE

BROCKWAY TRUCKS
1948 THROUGH 1961
PHOTO ARCHIVE

Photographs from the
Mack Trucks Historical Museum Archives

Edited with introduction by
Thomas E. Warth

Iconografix
Photo Archive Series

Iconografix
PO Box 609
Osceola, Wisconsin 54020 USA

Library of Congress Card Number 96-76225

ISBN 1-882256-55-7

96 97 98 99 00 5 4 3 2 1

Cover design by Lou Gordon, Osceola, Wisconsin

Printed in the United States of America

Book trade distribution by Voyageur Press, Inc. (800) 888-9653

PREFACE

The histories of machines and mechanical gadgets are contained in the books, journals, correspondence, and personal papers stored in libraries and archives throughout the world. Written in tens of languages, covering thousands of subjects, the stories are recorded in millions of words.

Words are powerful. Yet, the impact of a single image, a photograph or an illustration, often relates more than dozens of pages of text. Fortunately, many of the libraries and archives that house the words also preserve the images.

In the *Photo Archive Series,* Iconografix reproduces photographs and illustrations selected from public and private collections. The images are chosen to tell a story—to capture the character of their subject. Reproduced as found, they are accompanied by the captions made available by the archive.

The Iconografix *Photo Archive Series* is dedicated to young and old alike, the enthusiast, the collector and anyone, who like us, is fascinated by "things" mechanical.

ACKNOWLEDGMENTS

The photographs appearing in this book were made available by the Mack Trucks Historical Museum, which holds the Brockway corporate archives. We are grateful to Colin Chisholm, Curator, for his assistance.

Brockway factory, Cortland, New York, circa 1945. (PB226)

INTRODUCTION

Like Mack, of which it later became a part, Brockway originated as a New York carriage and wagon maker. The Brockway Carriage Factory was established in Homer, New York in 1851 by William N. Brockway. The first truck was built in 1910, and large contracts for World War I helped establish the company. Apart from a brief foray into the Midwest in the late Twenties, the company concentrated its efforts in the Northeastern United States. Brockway sold through mainly company owned dealerships, with headquarters and factory at Cortland, New York. US government military vehicle work further enhanced the Brockway reputation during and after World War II.

During the period covered by this book, Brockway sold from 1,000 to 2,000 trucks per year. On October 1, 1956 the company became an autonomous division of Mack Trucks, Inc., and in 1958 the Huskie line was introduced. The vehicles were largely hand-built from components supplied by others, such as Continental, Cummins, and Detroit Diesel, engines; Fuller, transmissions; Ross, steering gears; and Timken, axles.

The Brockway archives, from which these photographs were drawn, is held by the Mack Trucks Historical Museum. Images from the early part of the 1948 to 1961 period were plentiful, but far fewer remain from the later years. The photographs appear in roughly chronological order. Where possible, we give the negative number. It should be noted that dates do not necessarily correspond to the model year, however. A vehicle could have been new at the time of the photograph or it may have been in service for some time.

Specifications for all vehicle models were not available from the archive, nor were records explaining the significance of model suffixes. A sampling of specifications is listed in the appendix.

We hope that by presenting these fascinating images the reader will be encouraged into further research.

Model 154W, early 1948. (7502)

Model 146W, early 1948. (7505)

12

Model 152W, early 1948. (7517)

Model 260XW, early 1948. (7529)

Mixed fleet of Brockway trucks, early 1948. (7513)

Model 260XL, Summer 1948. (7549)

16

Mixed fleet of Brockway trucks, Summer 1948. (7552)

Model 154W, Summer 1948. (7556)

Model 128W, Summer 1948. (7562)

Model 260XW, Summer 1948. (7564)

Model 152W fleet, Summer 1948. (7590)

Model 260XW, Fall 1948. (7601)

Model 260XW, Fall 1948. (7602)

Model 88WH, Fall 1948. (7604)

24

Model 88WH, Fall 1948. (7618)

Model 148W, early 1949. (7648)

26

Model 260XW, early 1949. (7660)

Model 88W, early 1949. (7666)

Model 128W, early 1949. (7668)

Model 128W, early 1949. (7672)

Model 153W, early 1949. (7675)

Model 154W, Spring 1949. (7696)

32

Model 260XW instrument panel, Summer 1949. (7721)

Model 148W, Summer 1949. (7728)

Model 154WH, Summer 1949. (7737)

Model 128W, Summer 1949. (7733)

Model 128W, Summer 1949. (7735)

Model 154W, Summer 1949. (7739)

Model 260XW, Summer 1949. (7741)

Model 260XW, Summer 1949. (7750)

40

Model 260XW, Summer 1949. (7752)

Model M146, Fall 1949. (7775)

Model M152W, Fall 1949. (7802)

Model 151W, Fall 1949. (7800)

Model 151W, Fall 1949. (7804)

Model 260X, Fall 1949. (7805)

Model 260XW, Fall 1949. (7777)

Model 146W fleet, late 1949. (7816)

Model 128W, late 1949. (7817)

Model 154WD, late 1949. (7822)

Model 260XW, early 1950. (7827)

Model 260XW, early 1950. (7830)

Model 260XW, early 1950. (7831)

Model 260XW, early 1950. (7832)

Model 152Ws and 260XW, early 1950. (7837)

Model 152W, early 1950. (7838)

Model 154WH, early 1950. (7839)

Model 260X, early 1950. (7845)

Model 260X fleet, early 1950. (7846)

Model 260XW and 152W, early 1950. (7850)

Model 152W, early 1950. (7852)

Model 153W, early 1950. (7853)

Model 154W and 88WH, early 1950. (7857)

Model 154W, early 1950. (7870)

Model 146W, early 1950. (7871)

Model 260XW, early 1950. (7878)

Model 260XW fleet, early 1950. (7880)

Model 260XW, early 1950. (7885)

Model 146X, early 1950. (7888)

Model 153BB, Spring 1950. (7925)

Model 153BB, Spring 1950. (7898)

Model 153WBB, Spring 1950. (7905)

Model 240XW, Spring 1950. (7931)

Model 153BB, Spring 1950. (7951)

74

Model 152BB, Summer 1950. (7963)

Model M153BB, Summer 1950. (7967)

Model 153BB, Summer 1950. (7973)

Model 153BB, Summer 1950. (7975)

Model 154W, Summer 1950. (7978)

Model 152Ws and 152BB, Summer 1950. (7981)

Model M148W, Summer 1950. (7989)

Model 128W, Summer 1950. (7998)

Model 146W, Winter 1953. (8269)

Model 260XW, Spring 1954. (8452)

Model 151W, Fall 1954. (PB289)

Model 148SLs, Summer 1955. (8604)

Model 255W, Summer 1955. (8651)

Model 151WD, Fall 1955. (8665)

Model 154B school bus, Fall 1955. (8666)

Model 255W, Fall 1955. (8696)

90

Model 128WX, Fall 1955. (8714)

Model 260WD, Fall 1955. (8717)

Model 155W, Fall 1955. (8722)

Model 148WD, Winter 1956. (8732)

Model 255W, Winter 1956. (8733)

Model 260SQ, Winter 1956. (8736)

Model 154B school bus, Winter 1956. (8738)

Model 254W, Winter 1956. (8741)

Model 155W fleet, Winter 1956. (8743)

Model 255W, Winter 1956. (8745)

Model 255Ws, Winter 1956. (8759)

Model 255W, Spring 1956. (8767)

Model 88WHX, Spring 1956. (8769)

Model 260SQ oil field special, Spring 1956. (8776)

Model 260SQ oil field special, Spring 1956. (8770)

Model 260SF oil field special, Spring 1956. (8784)

Model 260SF oil field special, Spring 1956. (8779)

Model 260SF oil field special, Spring 1956. (8785)

Model 260SQ with bed, Spring 1956. (8788)

Model 256W, Spring 1956. (8796)

Model 255W, Spring 1956. (8809)

Model 256W propane, Spring 1956. (8801)

112

Model 128WX, Spring 1956. (8808)

Model 258W, Spring 1956. (8810)

114

Model 155W, Spring 1956. (8811)

Model 258W, Spring 1956. (8818)

116

Model 148WD, Spring 1956. (8824)

Model 148WD, 1959. (8824)

118

Huskie Model N260L, 1959. (9045)

Huskie model hauling Atlas missile components, 1960. (9352)

(9355)

Huskie Model 158, late 1961. (9743)

122

(9746)

Assembly line, 1958. (8997)

124

SELECTED SPECIFICATIONS

Model	147T	155W	158T
Year	1961	1960	1961
Gross Vehicle Weight	45,000 lb.	55,000 lb.	60,000 lb.
Engine	41BD	42BD	44BD
Cubic Inches	363	427	478
Brake Horsepower @ rpm	150 @ 3,200	165 @ 3,000	200 @ 3,000

Model	257	258T
Year	1960	1959
Gross Vehicle Weight	65,000 lb.	65,000 lb.
Engine	48BD	48FD
Cubic Inches	572	572
Brake Horsepower @ rpm	230 @ 2,800	230 @ 2,800

Note: All above engines are six-cylinder gasoline Continentals

The Iconografix Photo Archive Series includes:

The Iconografix Photo Archive Series is available from direct mail specialty book dealers and bookstores worldwide, or can be ordered from the publisher. For additional information or to add your name to our mailing list contact:

Iconografix
PO Box 609/BK
Osceola, Wisconsin 54020 USA

Telephone: (715) 294-2792
(800) 289-3504 (USA)
Fax: (715) 294-3414

Book trade distribution by Voyageur Press, Inc., PO Box 338, Stillwater, Minnesota 55082 USA (800) 888-9653
European distribution by Midland Publishing Limited, 24 The Hollow, Earl Shilton, Leicester LE9 7N1 England

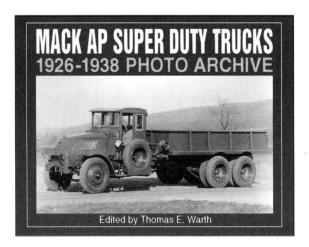

MACK AP SUPER DUTY TRUCKS
1926-1938 PHOTO ARCHIVE

Edited by Thomas E. Warth

MORE
GREAT BOOKS FROM
ICONOGRAFIX

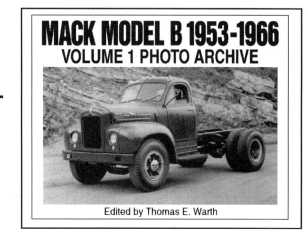

MACK MODEL B 1953-1966
VOLUME 1 PHOTO ARCHIVE

Edited by Thomas E. Warth

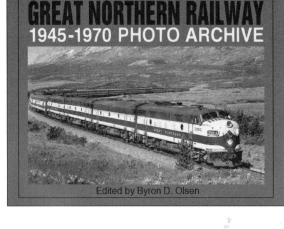

GREAT NORTHERN RAILWAY
1945-1970 PHOTO ARCHIVE

Edited by Byron D. Olsen

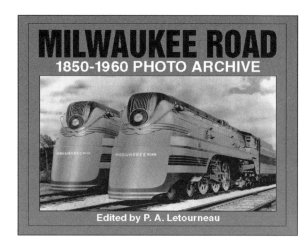

MILWAUKEE ROAD
1850-1960 PHOTO ARCHIVE

Edited by P. A. Letourneau

LOGGING TRUCKS
1915-1970 PHOTO ARCHIVE

Donald F. Wood

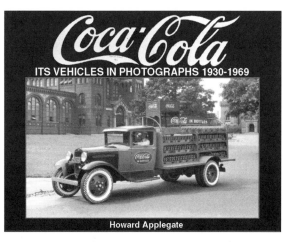

Coca-Cola
ITS VEHICLES IN PHOTOGRAPHS 1930-1969

Howard Applegate

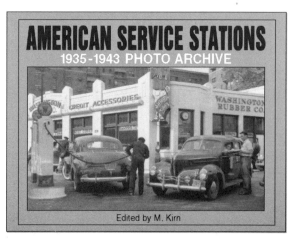

AMERICAN SERVICE STATIONS
1935-1943 PHOTO ARCHIVE

Edited by M. Kirn